A History of the Kitchen

A History of the Kitchen

DAVID J EVELEIGH

SUTTON PUBLISHING

First published in the United Kingdom in 2007 by
Sutton Publishing, an imprint of NPI Media Group
Limited · Cirencester Road · Chalford · Stroud ·
Gloucestershire · GL6 8PE

British Library Cataloguing in Publication Data
A catalogue record for this book is available from the
British Library.

ISBN 978 0 7509 4730 5

Typesetting and origination by
NPI Media Group Limited.
Printed and bound in England.

Contents

Introduction

A cheap shilling edition of Mrs Beeton's famous cookery book dating to the 1880s includes four lists of kitchen equipment graded according to the size of the house. The first is for any mansion. Everything imaginable is covered - from an eight day striking clock down to the rolling pin – at a total cost of £96 2s 4d. The second and third lists are for medium and small houses and the fourth, valued at just £7 13s 3d, covers the equipment necessary for the smallest house. The size and type of house, the social position of the householder and their means largely determined how the kitchen functioned within the home and how it was furnished. There were, inevitably, major differences between the kitchens of a mansion and a small dwelling. The kitchen of any large house was at the heart of a range of service rooms: it was a working environment for the servants who formed a separate and distinct community – albeit under the same roof – from the family. At the poorest level, the kitchen was often the only living space available and so everyday family life, cooking and washing took place in the one room.

The key is the house type and in this short book I have chosen to look at kitchens in this context. Most studies of kitchen equipment run chronologically or are structured according to the various cooking operations. But here, I have chosen to look at kitchens in farmhouses and cottages, mansions in town and country and in suburbia from early Victorian times to the 1930s. There is still an element of chronology in all three sections of the book although the dates attached to the chapter headings, are included simply to provide an approximate guide to the scope of each chapter. My chief aim is to explore the background to the kitchens in these three environments, to identify their particular characteristics – their function within the household – and also to capture something of their atmosphere, to provide the human dimension to the history of kitchen stuff. The book, therefore, features some of the people who lived and worked in kitchens - cooks, kitchen maids, farmhands and suburban housewives.

There were inevitably, common characteristics to the interiors, furnishings and equipment of the kitchens featured here. Fireplaces, sinks, large tables and clocks occur in all three sections. As in Mrs Beeton's four lists, there are overlaps but some topics lend themselves to particular chapters. Thus the rise of labour saving domestic machinery from the 1840s is described in the context of the Victorian middle class household although knife cleaners and other domestic machines were also to be found in the largest of kitchens. The development of the kitchen fireplace, however, runs through all three sections.

Within the confines of this little book it has proved impossible to fully explore each house type and others have had to be excluded altogether. The book is intended to serve as a taster to a more comprehensive study which I hope will follow. It draws on my own research and field work carried out since about 1980 but I have also drawn on the work of several leading food and domestic historians, particularly Peter Brears, Ivan Day, Pamela Sambrook and C. Anne Wilson. Any errors, however, in the concept or the detail, remain my own.

CHAPTER 1

Farmhouse and Cottage Kitchens, 1600 to the present day

The farmhouse kitchen has long held a fascination for those searching for traditional values and ways of life. In 1792, Arthur Young (1741-1820), agriculturalist, traveller and writer, wrote with affection of the kitchens of substantial farmers in Suffolk and the 'central counties'. 'A large, roomy clean kitchen', he wrote, 'with a rouzing wood fire on the hearth and the ceiling well hung with smoked bacon and hams'. Young's ideal conveyed a way of living untouched by pretension and modern fads - of rustic simplicity – plain manners and plain but wholesome food. Farmhouse kitchens were cosy, comfortable and convivial. They inspired writers such as Gertrude Jekyll (1843-1932) and artists like Frederick

Daniel Hardy (1826-1911) and Helen Allingham (1848-1926) who found in their interiors much which was picturesque - and without artifice - in good taste. For these and other admirers, the same timeless atmosphere could be found in the cottages of the better-off sort of rural labourer and the kitchens of old country inns.

In remote rural locations, farmhouse, cottage and country inn kitchens maintained and preserved traditional ways of doing things. Some proved remarkably resistant to change: as recently as the 1950s, it was possible to enter the kitchens of some farmhouses in Devon and, in effect, step back two or three hundred years. Their large open fireplaces with pots hanging over an open fire would have been familiar to a seventeenth century Devon farmer and his family. As early as the 1780s, rural kitchens could appear decidedly old fashioned. Staying overnight in the 'Red Lion' in Bodiam on 17 August 1788, John Byng (1743-1813) observed that the inns of rural Kent still cooked over wood fires, noting in his diary that, 'a common cook here would not know how to manage a coal fire'. Inevitably, farmhouse and cottage kitchens were subject to change, however subtle and gradual. When Arthur Young was writing in the 1790s, his ideal farm kitchen was already under siege, at least in those prosperous southern and midland counties. He and other rural commentators like William Cobbett (1762–1835), the son of a Surrey farmer, wanted to see farmers and their families living in the kitchen and rubbing shoulders with their farm servants and outdoor workers. But the prosperous farmer – socially aware and ambitious – was turning his back on the kitchen and retiring to a more private parlour or drawing room furnished like any of a well-to-do town dweller with upholstered furniture, carpets and worst of all, a piano!

As Arthur Young had observed, farmhouse kitchens were generally spacious. The kitchen at Unstead Farm, Godalming, Surrey, described by Gertrude Jekyll in

1904, was thirty feet long and twenty feet wide, with a low ceiling and paved with stone slabs. One was deeply cut with a large 'W' and marked the position of the well ten feet deep. A water supply, of course, was vital to the running of any kitchen but the sink and pump, which drew water from a shallow well, was more usually found located in a back kitchen or scullery.

The kitchen was the hub of the farmhouse: here the preparation and cooking of meals went on side by side with every day family life. Drawing on her late Victorian childhood in Castle Top Farm near Cromford, Derbyshire, Alison Uttley (1884-1976) wrote in 'The Country Child' of the farm kitchen as, 'the heart of the house…full of doors and windows and old oak and people going to and fro'. Essential kitchen equipment and furniture was frequently jumbled up with working tools from the farm. A valuation of the furniture at Hallen Farm, near Henbury, Gloucestershire, made in March 1870, records such a seemingly random assortment. It included two 'elbow wood seat chairs', a dining table, a mahogany bureau, an oak oval table, a weather glass, a settle, coal box, paraffin lamp, two saws, a steel yard and pestle and mortar. There were also two clotheshorses and a 'wash trough'. By this date much country and kitchen furniture was made of deal, replacing the native hardwoods – oak, elm, ash and beech - traditionally favoured by the village joiner.

At Unstead Farm in 1904, a long table of deal, eleven feet five inches long and two and a half feet wide, ran down the middle of the room. Dressers were found in farmhouses from the seventeenth century and made of oak or elm although nineteenth century examples were more likely to be made of deal or pine and painted or grained. Some dressers were built in as fixtures but many were moveable pieces of furniture. Alison Uttley's were of oak and consisted of 'shining brasses and beeswaxed sides and drawers with their own distinctive names'. The shelves above were filled with a dinner service, jugs of various kinds and a set of graduated dish covers. Other typical pieces of furniture included corner cupboards and bread creels or bacon racks suspended from the ceiling.

Most farmhouse and cottage kitchens were furnished with a clock. When the stock and effects of Mr Cripp's farm at Bierton, near Aylesbury, was sold by auction in August 1796, the kitchen furniture included a thirty hour clock in a 'wainscot case' whilst the kitchen at Hallen Farm in 1870 contained an eight day clock. At the 'Bell Inn', in Aldworth on the Berkshire Downs, a long case clock with a brass dial and a 'bull's eye' glass showing the pendulum is fixed between two settles beside the large kitchen fireplace. The clock was made by a Reading maker, Ian Hocker, about 1760 and has quietly ticked away in the corner of this public house ever since.

Standing in front of the hearth, the settle served as a seat, a draught screen and store; many settles had cupboards in the back in which hams were hung and lockers under the seats for keeping hand tools. Settles gradually appear in household inventories from the 1620s when they were also found in town houses; however, by the eighteenth century, the settle was established as the archetypal piece of country furniture: eminently functional, locally made and untouched by fashion. Many curved round from the side of the fireplace to face the hearth, creating a cosy, warm and intimate environment protecting its occupants from the strong draughts pulled through the kitchen by the large chimney. Thomas Hardy (1840-1928) described the benefits of the settle in 'The Return of the Native', first published in 1878. 'Outside the settle candles gutter, locks of hair wave, young women shiver, and old men sneeze. Inside is paradise. Not a symptom of a draught disturbs the air; the sitters' backs are as warm as their faces and old tales are drawn from the occupant by the comfortable heat…'.

★   ★   ★

The focal point of the kitchen, of course, was the large open fireplace. They ranged in width from about five to nine feet, some three or four feet deep with an opening supported by a low brick or masonry arch or an oak beam about five feet from the floor. A shelf above the fireplace provided space for miscellaneous kitchen utensils and ornaments. A farmhouse kitchen scene by W.H. Pyne (1769-1843) of about 1790 shows the mantle shelf filled with an hour glass, a mole trap, a chamber candlestick, two coffee pots, a cream skimmer, meat chopper, a candlestick, candle snuffer and a tinder box. Tinder boxes were essential kitchen articles for making a light until the widespread introduction of friction matches in the 1830s when they quickly fell from use. A wooden rack was sometimes fixed above the chimney opening. Known as a 'clavy' in Dorset, it was chiefly for storing roasting spits and occasionally, an old musket or blunderbuss. Made of steel, spits were liable to rust so it made sense to keep them close to the fireplace – not only the warmest part of the house - but also the driest. For the same reason, salt was stored close to the fireplace. Amongst the kitchen hearth equipment in Mr Cripp's farmhouse at Bierton in 1796, lot forty two included: 'a fireshovel, bellows and salt box'. They were knocked down for just two shillings.

The chimney fireplace had become an essential architectural and structural component of farmhouses and cottages across much of Britain in the sixteenth and seventeenth centuries. Its introduction was gradual. Starting around 1500 in the south-east, the chimney had reached the north by 1700 but as late as 1900, the central hearth occupying the middle of the floor lingered on in crofters' cottages in the Orkneys. Nevertheless, in some localities the adoption of the chimney occurred quickly enough to be worthy of notice. In 1577, William Harrison, rector of Radwinter in Essex, wrote that old men in his village had seen many changes in their lifetime, including 'the multitude of chimneys lately erected'.

Burning wood, turf or peat, the fireplace was usually large enough for people to sit within the recess on low stools or benches. Here they could look up the wide flue and on a cold, frosty night see the stars or when the weather was wet, hit by a sooty splash of rain. A cavity in the wall – or 'loft' – for smoking bacon and hams was a common feature at roughly first floor level. Fallen branches, roots and hedge cuttings were burned along with bundles of slim poles of coppice wood bound up as faggots. Lighter brushwood was made into 'bavins' which were used to light fires and heat ovens. The best faggots were made of ash and in some Devon farmhouses, it remained a tradition into the mid-twentieth century to burn one on Christmas Eve; as each hazel bind disappeared in the flames, glasses were raised to make a toast. As faggots burned quickly a sizeable log – called a 'back-stick' in Devon – was placed across the back of the fire to keep the fire going. Wood smoke was required for curing bacons and hams. Coal could not be used – nor resinous woods – such as fir or pine. The outer bark of oak was best and in 1904, Gertrude Jekyll noted that in west Surrey, this rough bark was sold by tanners for sixpence a sack for smoking bacon.

The fire was made on the hearth and the faggots placed across a pair of wrought-iron firedogs. Larger and taller firedogs, generally known as andirons or 'cobirons', were made with hooks to support a roasting spit and some had cup-like supports at the top which served as trivets or stands for small vessels. In Writtle in mid-Essex, John Hillyard, a brick layer left, 'two cup cobirons' when he died in 1726. At South Molton, Devon, fire dogs were still on sale in the local ironmonger's in the early 1950s. Then in 1982, a farmhouse in Butts Hill Road, Woodley, Berkshire – which had been virtually engulfed by the outward spread of suburban Reading – was found scarcely touched by the twentieth century. In the kitchen, rusty and unused, but still intact was an open hearth containing a pair of fire dogs. Such is the immutability of some farmhouses.

Coppice wood was not cheap. In early nineteenth century Hampshire, a hundred faggots cost between twelve and twenty six shillings. The expense of fuel was a cause of distress for the rural poor in the nineteenth century – especially in counties such as Wiltshire where wood was scarce. Some cottage dwellers used cow dung for fuel. In Cambridgeshire in 1811, it was reported that the poor dried slabs of dung for use on their hearths. In some localities, the inhabitants were able to exercise rights of turbary to take turf and peat from heath and moorland. In west Cornwall, the cutting of hundreds of turfs and faggots of furze in late spring was an important part of the farming year. The average Cornish farm, according to A.K. Hamilton Jenkin in 1934, required a thousand faggots of furze and a similar number of squares of turf each year. On its own, furze burned too quickly so turf was put on top to produce a slow burning fire with the acrid reek characteristic of peat and turf fires. Some of them reputedly never went out – like the peat fire in the 'Wagon and Horses Inn', Saltersgate, near Pickering in North Yorkshire – which, in 1939, it was claimed, had burnt continuously for a hundred years. Keeping the fire in over night had several advantages. In Devon farmhouses, porridge for the next morning was placed in a pot over the fire and gently cooked through the night. Water could also be kept warm over the fire. It was also a source of light from which candles and lamps could be rekindled.

★   ★   ★

Cooking took place on the 'down-hearth' and staring into the smoky, soot blackened chimney recess it was usual to see at least one large iron vessel hanging over the fire. Some chimney openings contained a fascinating assemblage of iron gear – cranes, adjustable hangers, hooks and trivets for supporting utensils over the hearth. These items were not mass produced but made individually – usually in the village forge – of sinuous wrought-iron. With the odd scroll added here and there or with a deft twist of the hot metal, the smith created equipment that was not only supremely functional but naturally graceful and pleasing to the eye.

Alternatively, pots were simply hooked to a horizontal bar fixed in the chimney. At Higher Week Farm at Zeal Monachorum, near Crediton, Devon, down hearth cooking continued until about 1942. Three crooks hung from a fixed bar: one held a boiler filled with water drawn from an outside pump. A second was used for a large tea kettle to which a slender curving wrought-iron lever known as a 'handy maid' was fitted. By pulling the lever, the kettle tipped forward, enabling boiling water to be poured safely without having to take the heavy and soot covered kettle off its hook. The third hanger – they were called 'crooks' in Devon – was occupied by a pot for heating water for the wash boiler or, alternatively, a three legged 'crock' was used to make stews, soups or boiled suet puddings.

In 'The Old Curiosity Shop' by Charles Dickens, Little Nell sought shelter in 'The Jolly Sandboys' – a 'roadside inn of ancient date'. There was a blazing fire spreading a ruddy glow around the room and a large iron cauldron hanging in the massive chimney opening which contained a stew of tripe, cow heel, bacon and steak with peas, cauliflowers, new potatoes and sparrow grass, 'all working up together in one delicious gravy'. When the landlord stirred the fire and lifted the lid of the pot, 'there rushed out a savoury smell while the bubbling sound grew deeper and more rich and an unctuous steam came floating out, hanging in a delicious mist above their heads…' That was 1842. Two years later, Mrs Parks, writing in Webster's 'Encyclopaedia of Domestic Economy', declared the three legged pot to be virtually redundant – except for boiling pitch - and use in the distant northern of Scotland. Yet according to Flora Thompson (1876-1947), in the 1880s, the inhabitants of her north Oxfordshire hamlet near Banbury still cooked a meal in the one iron pot over the fire. 'About four o'clock, smoke would go up from the chimneys as the fire was made up and the big iron boiler, or the three legged pot, was slung on the hook of the chimney'. Everything was cooked in the one utensil – potatoes, green vegetables and the meat – usually pieces of bacon – were placed in the pot in separate nets or cloths.

Other cooking operations could be carried out on the down hearth using specially adapted equipment. Frying pans were hung over the fire or made with long straight handles so they could be manipulated at a safe distance from the fire and without bending over. Cooking at hearth level could be back breaking so cooks often sat on low stools in the chimney opening. Pans were supported on a low tripod stand called a 'brandis'. In Devon the brandis was used to support a large pan of simmering water in which a covered jar of cream was placed to make clotted cream. When a skin of clotted cream had formed, it was taken off the heat and the cream skimmed off once it had cooled. In some parts of the country, chiefly in Wales and the north, oat cakes were made by spreading a batter of oatmeal mixed variously with yeast, bicarbonate of soda, water and salt, on a thick round, cast-iron plate

– a 'griddle' - heated over the fire. Some griddles were made with bail handles so they could be hung from a pot hanger. Mulled beer was warmed using small cone or boot shaped vessels of tin-plate or copper which were pushed into the fire until the beer had acquired a delicious creamy froth.

Dishes were also roasted, toasted and broiled over the hearth fire. Gridirons for broiling small pieces of meat were common in seventeenth century farmhouses along with roasting spits and dripping pans. Turning the roasting spit by hand was a hot and tedious task so the spits were often connected by an endless chain to a dog wheel, a drum-like wooden wheel, which was driven by a dog placed inside. One survives today in the 'George Inn' at Laycock, Wiltshire. From the 1660s, many rural householders of middling status turned to mechanical roasting jacks. Driven by a descending weight – like the movement of a long case clock - the jack usually occupied a conspicuous position at one end of the chimney mantle piece and the simple mechanism with its worm and flywheel was often placed behind a decorative front plate of brass. To extend the time of going, systems of pulleys which lengthened the travel of the weight, were often installed: the 1729 inventory of Margaret Hayward's farmhouse at Writtle, Essex, included a 'jack, pullies and weights' in her hall kitchen. Very few jacks survive in their original position but it is still possible to buy jack chain in hardware shops in the twenty first century although few appreciate the original association with spit roasting. Meat was also 'roasted' in ovens or in baking kettles. At Hedgeland Farm, Cadbury near Exeter, a round baking kettle was used in the 1920s and 1930s for roasting rabbits with a rasher of fatty bacon. The kettle was inverted over an iron plate on the hearth and embers piled up around it. In Cornwall, A.K. Hamilton Jenkin reported that the baking kettle was used for all sorts of dishes including heavy cakes, pasties and pies. 'Occasionally', he wrote, 'when very large joints of meat had to be roasted, the crock itself would be inverted over the baking iron in place of the kettle'.

Most large scale baking and especially the baking of bread relied on the brick or clay oven which was a feature of many large farmhouse and cottage kitchens. They were fired from the inside and usually located at the back of the fireplace so that the smoke and flames which came out of the mouth could be drawn straight up the main chimney. According to Hannah Glasse in 1747, the ideal shape for an oven was round and low roofed with a small opening so that it would heat up quickly and stay hot longer. Light brush wood was burned in the oven for about an hour until the interior had absorbed sufficient heat. Gauging the correct temperature was crucial to successful baking. It could be done by touch – extending an arm into the oven – or by throwing in some flour to see how quickly it browned or simply by watching the colour of the brickwork turn from black to red and then to white.

When it was ready, ash and any unburned wood was raked out and then the dough or other items placed inside using a long handled oven peel. The door was then closed and to conserve the heat it was often 'luted' with clay or sealed with thick, brown pasted paper. Separate, lift-off oven doors made from a thick piece of wood, such as horse chestnut, were once used and were doubtless effective heat insulators but from the eighteenth century, most doors came to be made of cast-iron. Inside the oven, the contents were heated by vigorous radiation from the glowing domed roof above and from below by direct contact with the oven floor: this accounted for the difference between the compact bottom crust and the darker, bubble bearing top crust of an ordinary loaf of bread.

The home baking of bread lasted longest in the West Country and in the Eastern counties where it was the staple diet in cottages. In Suffolk, every cottage housewife was taught by her mother the art of mixing, kneading and oven firing. It took considerable time and physical strength and effort to mix and ferment and knead and shape half a bushel – or twenty eight pounds - of flour into loaves ready for the weekly bake. In one cottage in the village of Ashdon, near Saffron Waldon in north Essex, the dough was prepared in the kneading trough the night before baking and by morning the dough would have risen, forcing off the trough lid. From the seventeenth century, cloam or clay ovens, became common in the West Country. Production was centred on the north Devon pottery towns of Barnstaple, Bideford and Fremington and at Calstock and Truro in Cornwall. They were made in Truro until 1937 and some were still in regular use in Devon farmhouses into the 1950s when it is recalled that the 'roast dinner', cakes, bread or sponges would share the one oven; other dishes baked in these ovens included pasties and rabbit pies. Shallow cast-iron hearth ovens which were placed under the open fire were found in parts of the rural south and south west of England in the nineteenth century. Denning & Co, of Chard, Somerset, had three sizes available in their 1905 catalogue.

*   *   *

The fires went out on the last few open cooking hearths in the 1950s but the tradition had disappeared in some areas much earlier through the adoption of coal which required an iron container – a grate – in order to burn well. In areas close to collieries, the domestic use of coal dates back to the middle ages, possibly even earlier. In areas where coal was readily available the adoption of the grate was largely complete by 1700. Small grates, consisting of wrought-iron bars set between low hobs of masonry or brick were commonly found in cottages. Cooking vessels were placed directly on the fire or supported on trivets attached to the topmost fire bar while other vessels continued to be suspended from hangers. In the kitchens of farmhouses and inns the grates were larger so that meat could be spit roasted in front of the fire. By the 1770s, North Country iron founders were making kitchen grates with iron ovens heated directly by the fire and these soon found their way into the countryside. An inventory of 1812 for a farmhouse at Hankeloe near Nantwich, Cheshire, lists a kitchen grate, oven and boiler in the 'house place' along with an ash grate, fender and fire irons. The following year, John Farrey, writing of Derbyshire, reported that grates with ovens and 'square iron boilers' had, 'spread so amazingly that there is scarcely a house without these ovens, even of the cottages of the first class'.

From the 1840s, the expansion of the railway network brought coal and manufactured goods including cast-iron grates, ovens and ranges from the industrial north and midlands into remote villages and farmsteads. For romantics, the passing of the open hearth was a matter of regret and the kitchen range a dread symbol of a new age of industrial mass production.

In his poem, 'The Settle and the Girt Wood Vire', William Barnes (1801–86), the Dorset dialect poet, mourned the passing of the wood burning open hearth.

'But they've walled up now wi' bricks,
The vier Pleace vor dogs an' sticks,
An' only left a little hole,
To Teake a little grate of coals'.

But ranges had their own appeal Many of those found in farmhouses and cottages were made by the same market town iron founders who provided the farmer with his ploughs, chaff cutters and other essential pieces of agricultural equipment. The result was the perpetuation of a regional or 'vernacular' character to many ranges. Thus there were 'Midland' ranges – many with a characteristic curved cut-away to the front panels each side of the grate below a small oven and boiler. Midland ranges were long lived: one remained in daily use for cooking in a cottage near Congresbury, Somerset in the mid-1990s.

Travelling on foot through rural England in 1872, Richard Heath, a journalist, took shelter from a storm in a dalesman's cottage near Reeth in Swaledale. 'Instead of the ancient hearthstone and open chimney and turf fire as one sees in the south', he wrote, 'there was a modern grate, possessing every convenience, such as large ovens and boilers, while the pots were suspended by hooks of polished steel to a crane of the same material'. This was very probably a Yorkshire range with a large open grate flanked by a boiler and an oven above the level of the fire. This distinctive feature was probably a legacy from the eighteenth century when cast-iron ovens were fitted high on one side of the chimney recess. The ovens of Yorkshire ranges had good bottom heat and recognised as the best for pastry and bread baking. The chief drawback was the absence of a hotplate. Some cooks opened the oven and used its floor as a cooking surface but it remained common for tea kettles to be suspended from hooks or 'reckons' attached to a chimney crane or 'reckon-bar' made of polished steel. Similar ranges were found in the north-east of England and those around Tyneside commonly had circular oven doors as J.C. Loudon (1783-1843) noted in his 'Cottage, Farm & Villa Architecture' in 1833.

But another distinctive regional type of range emerged in the second half of the nineteenth century in the far south west. This was the Cornish range – or 'slab'- which was typically a small unit incorporating a cast-iron fireplace surround. The slab referred to the cast-iron hotplate which occupied the entire width of the opening, enclosing the fire and covering the oven and boiler either side. They were made in over thirty foundries in the county although the chief centre of production was Redruth where the names of eight makers have been recorded. Cornish ranges feature some of the most ornate cast decoration found on ranges anywhere in the British Isles. The side panels, canopy and oven door are often cast in high relief with various patterns including neo-classical motifs – acanthus leaves and classical figures - floral designs and the royal arms. The oven door latch was typically secured by a large spring consisting of a handsome wrought-iron scroll whilst a generous use of brass for oven door handles, maker's name plates and edge beading added to the overall decorative finish. The brass work was polished by proud householders until it sparkled against the soft sheen of the black leaded cast-iron.

★   ★   ★

The agricultural depression which took hold from the mid-1870s saw many old established farming families giving up farming for good and with them disappeared old farmhouse skills and traditions, like home baking, the making of butter, cider or beer and rush lights. In 1938, William Wood, a farmer in the Weald of Sussex looked back to the 'bygone days' of his youth in the 1870s when his father's farmhouse contained an 'immense' kitchen with a cavernous chimney and a 'slowly revolving roasting jack'. He recalled that 'rush candles' were made in his uncle's farm kitchen but by the 1930s, he reflected, only a few old men like himself remembered the old farmhouse ways. When a family left a farm the inevitable sale saw the dispersal of household goods which sometimes represented several generations of occupation by one family. Wood recalled as a boy the sale of his uncle's farmhouse in 1874 and seeing the old service of pewter scattered among the forks and rakes, ploughs and harrows.

Here and there, old farmhouse kitchens seemingly impermeable to the forces of change lingered on. Both open hearth cooking and many more ranges could still be seen in use in the 1950s. Some farmers had turned to using paraffin stoves like the 'Valor Perfection' and then in 1929 the range was given a new lease of life when the 'Aga', invented by Gustav Dalen (1869-1937), a Swedish scientist was introduced to Britain. With a thermostatic control regulating the draught and maintaining the heat at any required temperature, the 'Aga' was both economical and easy to use. Retailing at sixty guineas in 1930, they were beyond the means of most suburban dwellers but they soon acquired a strong association with the countryside. As early as 1936, a farmhouse kitchen illustrated in 'Studio' magazine featured an 'Aga' in the old fireplace opening.

The farmhouse kitchen lives on but not necessarily in the countryside. It has now become a recognisable style of décor and a type of cooking adapted to the ceramic hob and the microwave cooker. The food is traditional and the decorative treatment is also retrospective with furniture of old pine or English hard woods: a large table, a dresser and Windsor chairs and ideally a solid fuel cooker – not an old range, of course, but an 'Aga'. So the farmhouse kitchen survives - albeit subtly modernised - a lifestyle option for those, like Arthur Young over two hundred years earlier, hankering after tradition.

CHAPTER 2

The kitchens of Mansions and other large Establishments, 1700 -1939

In September 1833, Walcot House, a large house overlooking the London Road in Bath was sold by auction. Standing in its own grounds, the auction particulars described it as, 'a most comfortable and gentlemanly residence'. It had a handsome entrance hall, a bow fronted dining room, a study and large drawing room. The basement contained beer and coal cellars, cellars for port wine and Madeira, a housekeeper's room, a 'spacious brew house' and 'a good roomy kitchen with area, steps and back entrance, improved smoke jack and range, stew holes, dresser and shelves'. The adjoining scullery had a stone trough and water supply.

These particulars could be repeated for many large houses in both town and country in the eighteenth and nineteenth centuries. They highlight the basic separation between the domestic offices with the kitchen at its centre and the polite parts of the house, typical of all large houses, regardless of location. In fact, the kitchens of large town and country houses were remarkably similar so far as their general layout and equipment was concerned. Many wealthy landed families were equally at home on their country estate or in town. Many had a London residence and when they stayed there for the season, some of their servants – including the cook – usually went with them. Others spent part of the year in Bath - like the fourth Duke of Bedford and Pitt the Elder, the Earl of Chatham, who, in the 1760s had homes in The Circus, begun by John Wood the Elder (1704-54) in 1754. In Scotland, wealthy country families relocated to Edinburgh for the season. From the late eighteenth century, there was nothing 'rustic' about the character of a well run country house kitchen. The range, ovens and other equipment was as likely to be purchased from a prominent London furnishing ironmonger, such as Clement Jeakes of Great Russell Street or Benham & Sons of Charing Cross than any local supplier.

There were, however, differences in scale, site and location. Walcot House was typical of town houses in having the entire service area located in the basement. Space in urban areas was always at a premium and even large houses were generally built on restricted sites with narrow street frontages. Instead they went up – and down – and usually the entire suite of domestic offices was relegated to the basement. The service rooms and the servants, therefore, were largely invisible but their presence could be felt in other ways. In the 1830s the Duke of Devonshire complained of the all-pervading smell of 'fry and fat' from the downstairs kitchens of the typical Brighton town house. Most town house basement kitchens – by day or artificial light - presented a sombre appearance. Ceilings could be relatively low and vaulted – like those of houses in The Circus, Bath. The few windows provided some light but little or no view. The main kitchen tended to be at the front and so its window faced the wall of the 'area' below street level. The area steps from the street provided the usual means of access for the servants and visiting tradesmen. At the rear a window in the back kitchen often looked onto a dreary back yard.

Large country estates generally offered more space for service areas and as a result there was more variety in the site and location of the service wing. Many were built at ground level, placed discretely to the north of the main block. Some large eighteenth century kitchens were actually detached which was an effective way of reducing the risk of fire as well as ensuring that smells and noise would not penetrate the family apartments. But against such advantages had to be balanced the inconvenient distance from the dining room. At Uppark, West Sussex, a separate kitchen, built in the early nineteenth century, was linked to the house by an underground passage. Occasionally, basement service areas are found in large country houses: the kitchen at Stourhead, Wiltshire, is underground and with its vaulted ceilings lined in sanitary white glazed bricks has a mortuary-like ambience. Sir Roger Pratt (1620-84), England's first architect knight, advised that the kitchen with all its offices should be placed in a half basement so that, 'no dirty servants may be seen passing to and fro by those who are above, no noises heard and no ill scents smelt'. At Castle Drogo, north Devon, designed by Edwin Lutyens (1869-1944), the service rooms are situated in a lower ground floor and lit from above. Typically, country house kitchens were spacious, well provided with daylight from windows or ceiling lights and lofty. The kitchen at Lanhydroc House, Cornwall, rebuilt after a fire in 1883, has its own impressive open timber roof resembling a college hall; clerestory windows in the roof could be opened by a system of rods and gears to improve the ventilation. At Castle Drogo, the kitchen is equally spacious and lit by a central lantern light in a high vaulted ceiling.

The domestic offices of many large country houses contained a greater range of service rooms than the town equivalent. Besides a scullery, some included a separate pastry, a brew house, a still room and dairy. In 1710, the contents of the pastry at Dyrham Park, Gloucestershire, included twenty one patty pans, cake and pasty pans, three earthenware potting pans for venison, two rolling pins and boards, an oven peel and 'a wooden gelly frame'. At Lanhydroc there is a separate bakehouse, containing an oven and prooving oven by Clement Jeakes. Then there were specialist stores and offices such as the game larder, the butler's pantry and housekeeper's room. The back kitchen or scullery of large establishments usually contained another range, several sinks, pumps and a wash copper which could be used for boiling large joints of meat, suet puddings as well as for the household wash. A reliable water supply was a vital part of any large dwelling. Mains water supplies were rare before the mid-nineteenth century and so each house had to have its own independent supply. One source was spring water which was drawn from brick-lined wells usually no deeper than thirty feet, the maximum depth at which a common iron suction pump could function. Spring water was – in theory, at least - relatively pure and safe to drink but it was usually hard and not suited to laundering purposes as it caused soap to curdle. For doing the weekly wash and for other scullery uses, rainwater was used and so many good quality houses had large rainwater storage tanks in the basement from which the water was again drawn by a hand pump.

The floors of large working kitchens were generally stone flagged. Walls were usually painted cream although some, as at Erdigg Hall, Clwyd, were a deep blue – a colour which is, apparently, repellent to flies. Skirtings, door and window frames were often finished in a dark brown whilst the furniture including the dresser was usually cream or buff – or 'drab'. Dressers of deal were always fitted and often located opposite the fireplace. An inventory of Attingham Hall, Shropshire, drawn up in 1913, records three: the largest having a deal top, five drawers and five cupboards. Some had an open lower course occupied by a pot board for the storage of large pots and pans, trivets and spare coal scuttles. The narrow shelves above the dresser board were used either for the display of dinner plates or copperware. A long table usually dominated the centre of the floor space. In 1913 the kitchen at Attingham contained a table, fourteen feet long and four feet wide with a thick elm top, a painted frame with eight legs and stretchers and two drawers. The kitchen also contained a flap table which folded away when not in use and another smaller table six feet by just over three feet; there were also nine lath back stained walnut Windsor chairs and another with arms. The Victorian kitchen table at Lanhydroc, which is still in situ, has drawers down the sides and at the cooler end, away from the heat of the kitchen fire, there is a marble top for working, rolling and trimming pastry. Other larger items included large mortars set in free standing wooden frames, moveable plate warmers which also doubled as fire screens and when the Prince Regent (1762-1831) had the Great Kitchen built at Brighton Pavilion in 1816, it originally contained a large oval steam heated table. Clocks were important, too. At Brighton Pavilion, the original clock retains its original position high on the wall above the shelves of highly polished copperware.

★　★　★

The Prince Regent was immensely proud of his kitchen and took particular delight in showing it off to visitors. On one occasion he even dined there with his servants, having a red cloth laid upon the floor. Other mistresses might inspect their kitchens to check that everything was in order but the kitchens of large establishments were part of a working environment that was separate - socially as well as physically - from the family parts of the house. This was the world of the servants and in particular, of the cook and the kitchen assistants. In large establishments the cooks were 'professed' - and the best were French - like Marie-Antoine Carême (1784-1833) - the inventor of caramel - who was brought over to work in the Brighton Pavilion in 1816. In January 1817, he prepared a splendid dinner there for the Grand Duke Nicholas of Russia, later Tsar Nicholas I. There were over a hundred dishes on the menu with 'La ruíne de la mosquée turque' and 'L'hermitage chinoise' among the 'grosse pièces de patisserie'.

Most other cooks were women and were assisted by one or two kitchen maids and a scullery maid. The duties of the assistants varied according to the size of the household. The first kitchen maid was usually expected to roast and boil meats and do most of the plain cooking and where there was a second kitchen maid, her duties would typically include the dressing of meat, poultry and vegetables. The duties of Margaret Thomas, who worked as a kitchen maid in a large house in Portman Square, London, around 1900, included waiting on the cook, cooking all the vegetables, roasts and savouries, making toast and coffee and doing all the cooking for the staff. She also did all the poundings and chopping, all the sieving and the washing up. Later, working in a country house in Yorkshire, she baked the bread twice a week. The scullery maid was at the bottom of the kitchen hierarchy and was responsible for the washing and scouring of the pots, pans and other utensils. 'Washing up was daunting' according to Eileen Balderson, recalling her time as a scullery maid at Rise Park, a country house near Hornsea, East Yorkshire, in the 1930s. She also had to peel the potatoes and if cooking salt was needed in the kitchen, she had to rub a seven pound block through a sieve: this was a painful job in winter when her hands were often chapped.

Scouring and polishing the copperware was a major task for the scullery maids. From the early eighteenth century, sheet copper cooking vessels began to replace utensils made of brass and other alloys of copper. By the mid-nineteenth century, most large kitchens contained an impressive 'battery de cuisine' of copper cooking vessels. These would typically include several types of stewpans, a braising pan, sauté pan, omelette pan, a fish fryer, a fish kettle, a mackerel pan, preserving pan, turbot kettle, a stock pot, a basin and a bain marie – a hot water bath for keeping sauces warm. Tea kettles, coffee and chocolate pots were also made of copper and an early reference to the use of these utensils is recorded in 1710 when the inventory of the Great Kitchen at Dyrham Park records two tea kettles of unspecified metal and two copper coffee pots. Copper pans were valued by all good cooks as the metal transmitted the heat from the stove or hot plate quickly and evenly. Copper was expensive and so a 'battery de cuisine' which included utensils of copper was a clear indicator of the wealth of the householder. They were often marked with the owner's initials or monogram: each item in the extensive battery de cuisine of copper vessels which belonged to the Duke of Wellington (1769-1852) at Apsley House, London, which is now on display in Brighton Pavilion – is marked 'DWL' for the Duke of Wellington, London. The copperware was invariably set out on the shelves of the dresser where it made an impressive display. In Portman Square, Margaret Thomas cleaned the various copper pans and moulds with a mixture of sand, salt and vinegar, and flour rubbed in by hand. 'Every morning', she recounted, 'when the Lady passed the slate [containing the menus for the day] in the servant's hall she came out to see them, and if one was missing inquired why it was not in its place'. But copper had one major disadvantage. It was soon discovered that acids naturally occurring in many foods reacted with the metal to produce highly poisonous verdigris which can cause severe illness and even death, so from the mid-eighteenth century, copper utensils were tinned on the inside to protect the metal. The only exception were preserving pans which could not be tinned as the boiling point of sugar is too close to the melting point of tin.

The copperware also included ornamental moulds for both sweet and savoury dishes. At Petworth, Sussex, there were over two hundred copper moulds in the kitchen in the late nineteenth century. The copper jelly mould reached its apogee of development in the 1860s and 1870s when makers advertised a wide range of moulds for jelly and other cold sweet desserts. Patents were taken out for complex moulds such as the 'Belgrave' patented by Temple & Reynold of Cavendish Square, London, and the 'Alexander Cross' and 'Brunswick Star' moulds, registered in 1863 and 1864 respectively. They were manufactured by Benham & Froud of Chandos Street, Charing Cross, a firm which traced its origins to the 1780s. The use of these mould required some degree of skill and dexterity on the part of the cook but the results were quite spectacular with jellies presented to the table in contrasting colours and some – like the 'Belgrave' – with a centre filling of ice cream or blancmange. From the 1860s, such jellies were illustrated to great effect in colour by book publishers using the new printing process of chromolithography.

Another important skill for any cook or kitchen maid was roasting. Until the early nineteenth century, there was only one way to roast meat and that was on a spit in the radiant heat of an open fire. The meat had to be 'put down' to a nice clear, bright fire. In 1844, Mrs Parks wrote, 'managing the fire well so as to have it clear in front, to get as much as possible of the radiant heat, is essential to success'. To project the maximum radiant heat, the kitchen grates or ranges of large houses were shallow from front to back but high and broad across the front. A large cast-iron range made at the Bucklebury foundry, near Newbury, Berkshire, in 1809 survives in situ in the detached kitchen of Bucklebury Manor. It is of massive proportions. The grate is five feet wide and the cast-iron hobs a further foot each bringing the overall width up to seven feet. The grate is roughly a foot deep at the top but as the cast-iron fire-back slopes forwards the grate is only about six inches deep at the bottom. The date of manufacture is cast on the fireback.

Roasting ranges were usually fitted with two adjustable side cheeks which could be wound inwards or outwards by a rack and pinion to adjust the width of the fire. The cheeks were wound out to create a huge fire for open fire spit roasting but wound in afterwards to save fuel. The 'Housekeeping Book' of Susannah Whatman, written in 1776 when she lived at Turkey Court, Maidstone, Kent, instructed the cook to, 'keep as little fire in the kitchen as may be necessary, always winding up the grate after dinner'. The size of the fire could also be reduced by folding down the top front fire bar and this 'falling bar' provided a convenient resting place for utensils. Circular cast-iron trivets which could swing over the fire were usually fixed to the top of the cheeks and could support a saucepan or tea kettle. Large pots were suspended over the fire on hangers and chimney cranes which were often fitted each side of the chimney recess.

At the beginning of the eighteenth century, most roasting spits in large kitchens were probably turned by dog wheels or weight jacks. There was a dog wheel in the Little Kitchen at Dyrham Park in 1710, but during the first half of the eighteenth century, smoke jacks, which utilised the powerful hot draught drawn up the chimney, were widely adopted. A London source of 1747 referred to them as, 'of late invention' although Leonardo Da Vinci had illustrated one in his sketchbooks as early as the late fifteenth century. A smoke jack was listed in an inventory of the contents of Appuldurcombe Park on the Isle of White, made about 1780, and by this time they were found above most large roasting ranges.

They consisted of a horizontal circular iron fly or fan attached to a vertical iron spindle and placed in a circular contraction of the chimney throat about two feet in diameter. Bevel gearing transferred the drive to a long horizontal axle with wooden pulley wheels at its ends running across the front of the chimney breast; chains from these wheels could drive several spits simultaneously. Dangle spits – hooks - from which smaller pieces of meat or poultry could be roasted – were also rotated by gear wheels on the main axle. Unlike its weight driven counterpart, the smoke jack did not require periodic re-winding but they were difficult to clean and maintain. Most chimney sweeps made a speciality of this work. Until the employment of young boys as sweeps was prohibited by law from 1842, the master would generally send one of his young climbing boys up into the chimney to clean the mechanism. Sweeps were also employed as fire fighters and the diary of William Turner (1807-92), a footman at 6 Great Cumberland Street, Marylebone, who kept a diary for 1837 records an incident on 23 September when they had to be called for. 'The kitchen fire caught fire this morning which put us all in a stew. We sent for the sweeps and they soon put it out without any more to do.'

As large kitchen grates were not suitable for lighter cooking operations they were usually supplemented by an oven, stewing stove and sometimes a copper which would be used for boiling large pieces of meat and puddings. From about 1750, iron founders began to make cast-iron ovens which had their own firebox, flues and damper arrangement: they were known as 'perpetual ovens', probably because they could be kept hot for any length of time. They were made in various shapes, round or with an arched top, octagonal, square or completely circular and some were elaborately cast with decoration. The Carron Foundry, established near Falkirk, Stirling, in 1759, produced oven doors cast with high quality classical reliefs in the fashionable neo-classical style: these were probably the work of the brothers, James and Robert Adam who prepared designs for the company. In 1985, a handsome iron oven was discovered in the derelict kitchen of a large terraced house in Harley Place, Clifton, Bristol, completed about 1815. It was made by the Benthall foundry of Coalbrookdale, Shropshire, and the door is embellished with a profile bust of Admiral Howe (1726-99) taken from a Wedgwood medallion modelled by the French sculptor, John De Vaere (1755-1830) in 1798.

The stewing stove was required for the preparation of stews and sauces and introduced in the seventeenth century. It usually consisted of a brick structure containing one or more small separate grates for burning charcoal. Sir John Vanbrugh's 'Notebook for Kings Weston', Gloucestershire, contains a drawing, dated 1717, of a large stewing stove with three small grates although some late eighteenth century examples consisted of an iron hotplate heated by a single firebox.

Usually these extra facilities were placed either side of the range. The cooking facilities of a large country or town house thus presented an impressive spectacle, occupying the greater part of one wall of the kitchen with subsidiary flues from the oven, stewing stove and boiler running at an inclined angle to join the chimney throat above the range. Preparing a large meal including roast and boiled dishes, sauces and pies would have resulted, therefore, in three or four fires burning simultaneously in the kitchen, generating huge quantities of smoke, heat and ash and creating a hot and unpleasant working environment – especially in warm weather.

Roasting ranges with smoke jacks continued to be fitted into the kitchens of some large kitchens throughout the nineteenth century. When Colonel Blathwayte rebuilt the service block at Dyrham Park, about 1855, he chose to install a large roasting range, smoke jack and separate oven made by Stothert & Walker, iron founders in nearby Bath. As late as 1907, one was installed in the

Skinner's Hall, London: it is now an exhibit in the Science Museum, London. However, after 1850, kitchen ranges with ovens and a boiler were increasingly adopted in large establishments. They were either open to the chimney – like the traditional roasting range - or enclosed on top. As early as 1799, Count Rumford (1753-1814), an American soldier and scientist, had condemned the inefficiency of the open range. In an essay on the construction of kitchen ranges, he said, 'more fuel is frequently consumed in a kitchen range to boil a tea kettle than with proper management would be sufficient to cook a dinner for fifty men'.

Rumford, instead, advocated a cooking stove of brickwork – not unlike an ordinary stewing stove - with small separate fireplaces for each vessel. His stove was never adopted but it probably influenced the development of the closed range which was first patented just three years later. George Bodley, an Exeter iron founder, took out patent protection for a range with an enclosed fire in 1802, but closed ranges were more closely associated with the Midland spa town of Leamington where William Flavel (1779-1844), began their manufacture in the 1820s. He called them, 'Patent Kitcheners' and they quickly gained acceptance. Flavels won a prize for one of their ranges at the Great Exhibition in 1851 and then the 'Leamington Kitchener' was given a further boost in 1861 when Mrs Beeton wrote, '…the improved Leamington Kitchener is said to surpass any other range in use for easy cooking by one fire'.

The closed range made better use of the heat as the fire was covered over with a hot plate, forcing the hot draught through oven flues before being lost to the chimney. Moreover, the hot plate enabled more saucepans and other utensils to be kept boiling at the same time, kept them clean and as they were protected from the direct heat of the fire, they lasted longer. By the late nineteenth century, many large open roasting ranges had been replaced by modern closed ranges although the old separate iron oven often survived. When the disused kitchen of circa 1740 at Betchworth House, Surrey, was recorded in 1982, an eighteenth century iron oven made by Carron with an ornate octagonal door was found in situ. The low arched fireplace opening, however, contained a late Victorian closed range by Benham & Sons, six feet wide, with two ovens. At Castle Drogo, two anthracite burning 'Kooksjoie' ranges made by the London Warming Company were installed in 1927. In the following decade, the 'Aga' found its way into country house kitchens: a three oven 'Aga' was installed at Dunham Massey in 1938 and four oven models at Hardwick Hall, Derbyshire and Felbrigg Hall, Norfolk.

By the 1930s, many landed families were fighting a losing battle against declining incomes, rising taxation and rising costs. As servants became harder to find – and more expensive – families were forced to reduce the size of their households. In many instances, country estates were offered for sale. When the house at Aynhoe Park, Northamptonshire, was finally sold in 1960, the great kitchen was converted into a split level flat. But the fate of some houses was worse, ending up empty and derelict. The decline was not confined to the sale of country estates. After the First World War, magnates like the Marquess of Salisbury and Lord Dartmouth sold their London town houses and the inter-war period saw the disappearance of their society life in town: Mayfair was abandoned to hotels, flats and offices. Elsewhere, large town houses were split up into flats and bed-sits as once fashionable districts lost their social exclusivity. The kitchens were either left derelict or turned into basement – or 'garden' - flats. A few have been refurbished as museums – like Number 1 Royal Crescent in Bath - whilst in the countryside, the service areas of great houses and particularly their kitchens have become major visitor attractions in their own right.

CHAPTER 3

Kitchens in Town and Suburbia, 1850 -1939

The nineteenth century witnessed a massive expansion of Britain's urban population. At the mid point of the century, 54% of the population lived in urban accommodation. Between 1851 and 1911, the population doubled but the urban population increased three times: by 1911, 79% of the population were town dwellers and large areas of suburban housing had been created. Then after the First World War, a further massive expansion of English suburbia took place through the building of 1.6 million council houses and an even larger number of privately owned homes typified by the mock Tudor semi detached house.

The new Victorian suburbs built from the 1850s were sharply socially segregated with marked differences in the quality of the housing and the level of services provided. Working class housing was typically situated close to the places of work and consisted largely of rows of densely packed terraced houses. Individual houses were small and overcrowding was common. The prosperous middle classes, on the other hand, sought to escape the smoke and dirt of towns for life in new quiet residential areas. Large terraced houses, fashionable in the first half of the century, fell from favour after 1850: instead, the preferred house type was the substantial detached or semi-detached villa with sufficient space for servants to live and work separately from the family.

Privacy and domestic comfort were of paramount importance to the Victorian middle class household. Complete separation from the family rooms was considered essential. 'A good kitchen, wrote Mrs Beeton, in 1861, should be, 'sufficiently remote from the principal apartments of the house, that the members, visitors, or guests of the family, may not perceive the odour incident to cooking, or hear the noise of culinary operations'. As a consequence, most kitchens continued to be consigned to a basement or semi-basement service area – a gloomy gas lit world of the cook - on call to the family upstairs. A system of servants' bells was the usual means of communication between servant and employer. In 1860, the kitchen of Lavender Hill, Wandsworth – the home of George Kent (1810-90), a prominent London manufacturer of domestic machinery - contained '7 bells & carriages with wires complete from each room'.

The service area of a typical mid-Victorian villa included a kitchen, a scullery, a larder for the storage of fresh meat and a pantry. There were also stores for coal and wood and usually a separate servants' WC and in the largest, a housekeeper's room. Many substantial Victorian villas - like large establishments in town and country - maintained a clear distinction between the front or main kitchen where cooking took place and the back kitchen containing the water supply and fitted with at least one sink and a wash copper. In most towns, water remained a scarce and unreliable commodity until the spread of continuous supplies of mains water from the 1850s. In the mid-century, many town house kitchens remained dependent on spring water drawn from shallow wells or stored rain water. Shallow wells, however, were liable to contamination from leaking or overflowing cesspools and until the 1870s, were often the source of local epidemics of typhoid and cholera.

Notwithstanding the typical basement location, good ventilation and light were considered important if the kitchen was to function efficiently and the cook to keep her temper. Borrowed daylight was transmitted to the inner confines of the basement through windows in partition walls but gas light was the usual source of artificial light. The lights generally used in kitchens were known as flat flame burners. There were no fancy shades of etched glass, just a length of pipe of cast-iron or brass with a simple burner which produced a flat, yellow naked flame varying in shape according to the configuration of the holes in its end. Thus there were 'bats wing' and 'rats tail' burners but the commonest light was the 'union-jet' or 'fish-tail' burner. This had two holes drilled at an angle in the burner so that two streams of gas merged spreading the flame to something like the tail of a fish. Large kitchens were typically illuminated by a pendant light consisting of two burners suspended over the main work table. George Kent's kitchen at Lavender Hill in 1860 contained, '1 Gas Burner on Mantle Shelf' – another common arrangement.

The range and the dresser were landlord's fixtures but everything else in the kitchen had to be supplied by the family and in order to equip it fully, the householder was able to refer to a wide range of domestic manuals and cookery books. Eliza Acton, Mrs Parks, Mrs Rundell,

Mrs Beeton and Mrs Caddy and others provided the middle class reader with detailed descriptions and lists of the furniture, equipment and utensils essential to the smooth running of the kitchen. The most important item of furniture was a large deal table with a scrubbed top which was usually placed in the middle of the room under the gas light. Other items of furniture included smaller tables, a napkin press, clothes stands and a few Windsor chairs. There was also usually a clock. Mrs Beeton stressed the importance of punctuality of in the kitchen: meals would be expected on time in well run households. In the mid-nineteenth century, so-called 'Dutch' clocks with pretty hand painted wooden faces, a long pendulum and weights were common. These inexpensive clocks were made in Germany and, according to Mrs Parks in 1844, cost only twelve shillings but gradually, they gave way to eight day mahogany dial clocks.

A well equipped kitchen required a range of utensils

for a variety of cooking operations. Victorian cookery books contain many recipes for boiled meat for which large, oval bellied boiling pots of cast-iron were almost universal. Most other vessels used over the range in the middle class household were made of cast or wrought-iron and capable of withstanding heavy usage over an open coal fire. Broiling, roasting and toasting required a hot fire, clear of smoke. Apart from the largest of kitchen ranges, the relatively small grate of the typical Victorian kitchen range precluded the use of roasting on a horizontal spit, so instead, meat was suspended over the fire and rotated on a vertical axis with the aid of a clockwork bottle jack. The name came from their shape – like that of an ordinary glass bottle - and most were made of brass in Birmingham by firms like Salters and John Linwood. The jack was hooked to a specially made bracket of steel or brass called a jack crane which was screwed or clamped to the fireplace lintel. Alternatively, the jack could be used inside a shiny tinplate meat screen – variously known as a hastener or dutch oven which was placed close to the fire where the meat roasted within the bright interior free of cold draughts. The steady rotation of the meat – first one way and then the other - doubtless mesmerised the average kitchen cat, whilst the jack's slow tick reassured the cook - while she got on with other things – that the meat was on its way to be being 'done to a turn'.

The clockwork of the bottle jack took the drudgery out of roasting and was one of several labour saving devices available to the Victorian cook. Bottle jacks had appeared by 1790 but the era of labour saving domestic machinery did not get under way until the 1840s. The first device to make a major impact was the rotary knife cleaner, first patented by George Kent in 1844. This machine with its mechanical spring loaded brushes contained in a wooded drum-like case and turned by a crank handle was capable of scouring several steel knife blades at once. 'Time and Labor Saved' was Kent's slogan. It was a phenomenal success and the only item of domestic machinery to collect an award at the Great Exhibition in 1851. Within a year or two of the Great Exhibition, the rotary mincer had made its debut. By 1853, Nye & Company of Soho, London, were advertising a mincer, which, they claimed, could mince eight pounds of meat in four minutes; this was, they claimed, 'a little item which every husband ought to carry home to his wife'. The London firm of Spong & Company was established in 1856 and soon became famous for its mincers. Other devices followed. Nye & Co. patented a sausage machine in 1860 while Spong introduced a bean slicer and in 1884, the Manchester firm, Follows & Bate introduced their 'Magic Marmalade Cutter'. This did not make marmalade by magic or any other means but simply produced neat regular slices of orange or lemon peel for use in marmalade making. There were also mechanical apple peelers, raison stoners, vegetable slicers, suet choppers and rotary bread graters. But the verdict of some 'experts' was mixed. 'Mincing machines, apple paring machines and toys of this kind' observed Mrs Caddy in 1877, 'are all very well when ladies use them themselves; but they represent so much idleness, waste and destruction in the hands of careless cooks who like to sit over their letter writing or their weekly paper'. She added, 'By the time one has prepared the meat to feed the machine, set it in working order and taken it to pieces again to clean it one might as well have used a sharp knife'.

Domestic manuals invariably discussed the merits of the various kitchen grates or ranges available. The exposed fire of an open range was a useful aid to the cook, especially for broiling, roasting and toasting; it kept everyone cheerful but wasted most of the heat. Most writers recommended the closed range which was considered more efficient and cleaner. In the middle decades of the nineteenth century, one of the most successful models was the Leamington kitchener. As early as 1833, J. C. Loudon reported that open ranges had been, 'entirely laid aside in favour of kitcheners in villas around Leamington'. But Mrs Parks, for one, was inclined to reserve judgement on the closed range. 'For common English cooking and English servants', she wrote in 1844, 'we can scarcely venture to recommend dispensing with a good open fire'. She doubted if the claimed saving on fuel was actually offset by the initial high expense, and other inconveniences – such as their tendency to break down – and the necessity of frequent cleaning of the flues. Then there was the time and trouble, she said, involved in teaching a cook how to use a closed range. Nevertheless, she did concede that when the inside of the chimney was lined with white glazed tiles they had, 'a very neat and clean appearance'.

The closed range, of polished black lead and burnished steel and brass was an indispensable part of the Victorian middle class villa. Large models had separate ovens either side of the grate for roasting and baking and from the 1850s, they were increasingly fitted with sealed back boilers so they could also supply the modern villa with running hot water. With so many demands placed on such ranges, it was vital that the dampers were used correctly to direct the hot draught to where it was required but many cooks either did not appreciate this or, perhaps, simply were not prepared to bother. As the trade journal, 'The Ironmonger' observed in 1900, 'the proper way to work a kitchener is not taught at our cookery schools and where the teacher is an average cook it is tolerably safe to say that she does not know it herself'. Rather than close down the flues that were not in use it was easier to leave them all open. The result was a constant roaring fire, unmanageably hot ovens, unbearable heat and heavy fuel bills.

An obvious remedy was to slow down the rate of combustion by converting the enclosed grate into an open fire so the smoke bypassed the flues and instead passed directly into the chimney. In 1846, Joshua Harrison, a Derby grate manufacturer introduced the

'The Economical Derby Range' which, converted to 'a common open fireplace' when three fire doors covering the fire and a door in the chimney were opened. Others followed, including the 'Lichfield Range' manufactured by William Carter & Co. of Birmingham, patented in 1866. By the late nineteenth century, most closed ranges were made so they could be converted speedily into an open fire.

According to J.H. Walsh in 1857, in 'well appointed houses', an open range was often retained for the back kitchen where it served as an ancillary range – especially for open fire roasting - when a closed range was fitted in the main kitchen.[1] As late as 1904-5, the German architect, Hermann Muthesius (1861-1927), writing of English house design, acknowledged the importance of the open fire for two essentially English culinary specialities: roasting meat and the toasting of bread. 'The English', he wrote, 'are still very fond of roasting meat at an open fire' and in the 1907 edition of Mrs Beeton, the clockwork bottle jack for roasting meat was considered too familiar to warrant explanation.

By the mid–1880s, the range was facing serious competition from the gas companies. The price of gas halved in the second half of the nineteenth century and thanks to the development of the air enriched burner by Dr Bunsen from the mid-1860s, gas cookers burned with a hot blue flame. Advertisements aimed to overcome the innate conservatism of the average cook by demonstrating that gas cookers could do everything the best ranges could do – without the smoke and dirt, occupying less space and, if the gas companies were to be believed, at less cost. The gas companies took to hiring them out for a trifling weekly rent. Between 1850 and 1900, the price of gas halved and by 1885 there were about two million gas consumers in England and Wales and increasingly householders were using gas for cooking as well as lighting. By 1908 about 40% of households in Bristol, for example, had turned to cooking by gas. Where gas was not available, paraffin stoves, which appeared about 1870, offered another, albeit more limited challenge, to the coal burning range.

Servants were often the bane of middle class households but they could not do without them. The Victorian middle classes almost invariably employed live-in servants. The usual number was two or three and always included a cook. Most were 'plain' cooks who were only expected to serve plain, simple dishes with dinners consisting of fish, a joint of meat and vegetables followed by a pudding or tart and luncheons. Lunch would consist of either a joint or cold meat with vegetables. The cook usually had to work single handed with occasional help from the housemaid. Kitchen and scullery maids were rare. In 1871 in the affluent suburb of Surbiton in Surrey where 45% of 1,388 households had at least one servant, there were only twenty one kitchen maids and two scullery maids. Life for many plain cooks was often hard and frequently involved duties quite unconnected with the kitchen itself such as cleaning the front hall and door step. Hours were long and there was little freedom. As one cook of Surbiton Hill complained to the 'Surrey Comet' in July 1872. 'For all this slavery - for it is nothing else – I am rewarded by being let out one evening a week – a whole two hours – and Sundays the same'.

Some cooks though, had the upper hand and an experienced cook could even intimidate a young mistress. They could after all leave at short notice. Relations between employer and servants, therefore, were often tense and characterised by mutual suspicion: the master or mistress of the household demanded not only competence but also loyalty and honesty. The complicated employer-servant relationship was the subject of many humorous cartoons in the journal, 'Punch' which must have chimed with the real life experiences of many of its readers. Frustration with cooks lacking even basic culinary skills is brought to life in 'The Dairy of a Nobody' by George and Weedon

Grossmith, the fictional diary of Charles Pooter, which had originally appeared in 'Punch'. Pooter, a City clerk and resident of 'The Laurels', Brickfield Terrace, Holloway, records his exasperation with his servant, Sarah, who was both cook and general maid and incapable even of serving a hard boiled egg.

★   ★   ★

In the Victorian working class home, the specialisation of space was less marked than in the middle class villa and the level of services simpler. The typical plan of the industrial small town house was the 'two up two down' - just two main rooms on the ground floor - and two bedrooms above separated by the staircase. The back-to back houses of northern industrial towns like Bradford often contained just one ground floor room – the 'house' which served as kitchen and living room and a small scullery partitioned off at the rear or side. In through terraced houses, a small back kitchen or scullery was commonly located in a small extension projecting into the back yard. A fireplace flanked by a wash copper and stone sink were usually built into the rear wall of this room with a separate chimney stack from the main part of the house. The back parlour then became the main living space – sometimes called the kitchen - with the front room reserved for best. The provision of a scullery made it possible to banish washing from the living room. In 1900, Seebohm Rowntree (1871-1954), noted that in York the real living room was the kitchen, 'rendered cheerful and homely by the large kitchen grate and the good oven…where the thrifty housewife bakes her own bread.'. 'A sofa', he added, 'albeit of horsehair or American cloth, an armchair, a polished table and china ornaments on the high mantelpiece, add the subtle touch of homeliness'.

Between 1850 and 1900, the provision of basic services in working class housing improved hugely. In 1851, Prince Albert encouraged the use of kitchen ranges in his model labourers' cottages built in South Kensington for the Great Exhibition but it is clear that most mid-

Victorian working class kitchens had no cooking facility other than a simple open grate set between masonry hobs. By 1900, however, a kitchen range was virtually a standard builder's fitting in the working class town house. They were small – some just thirty inches wide – with a tiny oven but no boiler. 'Portable ranges' which were, in effect, free standing cooking stoves on legs and with a stove pipe connection to the chimney flue were also commonly fitted in terraced houses built in the 1890s and early 1900s. Later nineteenth century working class housing was supplied with mains water although the supply was usually confined to a single cold tap over the sink. Following the introduction of fireclay sanitaryware by Francis T. Rufford of Stourbridge in 1850, fireclay sinks - typically finished with a buff glaze – came to replace the old stone sinks. Known variously as 'Edinburgh', 'Dublin' and 'Belfast' sinks, they were considerably more hygienic than those of stone which required constant scouring if they were not to acquire an unwholesome green patina.

By the late nineteenth century, most small terraced houses were also fitted with gas lighting and the kitchen was usually provided with a swing bracket fixed on the mantle shelf. From 1885, gas lighting was improved following the development of the incandescent gas light by an Austrian, Baron von Welsbach (1858-1929). The oxides of two rare metals, thorium and cerium, placed on a flimsy cotton mantle, were heated to incandescence by a hot blue flame. The incandescent gaslight was at least ten times more efficient than conventional burners and by 1920 had rendered the old flat flame burners virtually obsolete. The introduction of the penny-in-the slot meter from the late 1880s enabled poorer families to pay for the gas in small affordable sums as they went along. At about the same time, many gas companies began to hire out gas cookers on cheap weekly rents and this brought gas cooking within the reach of the urban working class household. By 1914, the use of the coal burning range in working class town houses was rapidly giving way to cooking by gas.

★   ★   ★

The First World War marked a watershed in British house construction. For the first time, the large-scale provision of working class housing became the responsibility of the state whilst the building of middle class homes for owner occupiers was subject to new pressures such as the arrival of electricity and the apparent shortage of servants. The building of both the new council estates and the development of middle class suburbs by private developers in the inter war period was heavily influenced by the Tudor Walters Report published by the Local Government Board in 1918. Drawing on the Garden City movement and expert opinion from specialist groups including women's organisations, entirely new house types were created.

The deep narrow frontages which characterised

Victorian town housing were condemned. Instead, houses were to have wider frontages in the 'garden suburb vernacular' style and rear extensions which cut off light and air were abandoned. The kitchen now had to be squeezed into an almost square ground floor plan. As a consequence, many kitchens – or sculleries – the distinction was now beginning to blur – were smaller than ever. A new concept – or at least a new name arrived: the 'kitchenette'. The first wave of council houses built in London – some 8,799 in total – contained a living room and a kitchenette measuring eleven feet nine inches by six feet three inches. These particular houses contained a separate bathroom but many early council houses had a bath in the scullery, an idea which had been mooted by the Local Government Board as early as 1912. To save space some baths folded vertically to fit in cupboards whilst others were covered with table tops when not in use. In 1918, 150 houses for munitions workers were erected on the Penpole Estate near Avonmouth, Bristol. They contained a small scullery just six feet deep and between the white fireclay sink at one end and a cast-iron bath at the other, there was just enough space for a small wooden drain board, a wash copper and gas cooker.

A similar arrangement was found in the many council houses built to the 'non parlour' plan. These had one main living room containing a cooking range and a separate scullery with a sink and copper. The ranges were usually combinations of conventional living room fireplaces and ovens which were finished in bright enamel or coloured tiles – like the 'Triplex' and 'Yorkist'. But an enquiry into new houses carried out in 1923 by the Women's Committee of the Garden Cities and Town Planning Association, noted a growing tendency to use the living room/kitchen purely as a sitting and dining room. Instead, cooking was done with all other work in the scullery using a gas cooker and rendering the combination range an expensive anachronism.

Middle class housing built between the wars, typified by the three bedroom semi-detached house, was markedly smaller in scale than its Victorian and Edwardian predecessors. There was no longer a separate service area and while some houses were built with a single storey rear extension containing a kitchen and larder, many followed the layout of council houses in having small kitchenettes or sculleries. They were sold to their buyers as 'labour saving' although the reduced scale of the kitchens - and the houses themselves - was largely the consequence of cost cutting by the builders. Nevertheless, saving labour was an important consideration for the rapidly expanding property owning but largely servantless middle classes of the inter-war period. The family – and particularly the housewife - were now faced themselves with the 'daily household round'. Writers such as R. Randall Phillips, the editor of 'Homes & Gardens', first published in 1919, explored ways that housework could be minimised by planning and equipping rooms to avoid unnecessary labour.

Inevitably, the kitchen came in for particular scrutiny. The large Victorian kitchen with its range and dresser and separate scullery was condemned as out of date and inconvenient. R. Randle Phillips promoted the idea of the kitchen-scullery where everything was 'ready to hand'. Convenience, cleanliness and lightness and efficiency were the guiding principles governing the design of kitchens and their equipment between the wars. Considerable attention was placed on the relationship between the cooker, sink and food preparation to minimise unnecessary movement. For the housewife who was now likely to be both hostess and cook, it was considered best to locate the kitchen next to the dining room, with the two rooms linked by a serving hatch. As the housewife had to spend more time herself in the kitchen, writers suggested the room should be 'bright and cheerful' with tiled floors covered in linoleum or cocoa-nut matting and walls painted with pale washable paint: cream, light blue and 'eau de Nile' – a pale green - were popular choices.

From the early 1920s, kitchen cabinets which had originated in America began to replace the traditional dresser. Portable and free standing, the kitchen cabinet consisted of a compact arrangement of cupboards and shelves with a folding out work table and special containers for various kitchen utensils and stores such as tin lined drawers for bread and a flour hopper. Bringing a large number of things together, the kitchen cabinet saved on unnecessary movement. A further labour saving consideration was that their fronts were made without mouldings in the 'modern dust proof style'.

Similarly, the use of gas for cooking and water heating was promoted as more convenient and cleaner – and, therefore, labour saving – than the solid fuel range even though gas was still more expensive than coal. Cleaning the range, increasingly, was seen as an unnecessary chore. New houses built from the early 1920s in the new suburb of North

Harrow by Albert Cutler, a local builder, were provided with coke fired boilers in the kitchen for independent water heating. These, he claimed, 'are rapidly superseding the old-fashioned, dirty and wasteful kitchen range'. From the early 1920s, the design of gas cookers was improved. They were made of lightweight enamelled sheet steel which was easier to keep clean; the oven was also raised from the floor to a more convenient height. Improved burners were introduced providing better control of the gas ring and one of the most important innovations was the introduction of 'Regulo' oven thermostatic control by Radiation Ltd in 1923. It was an invaluable aid to the hard pressed housewife allowing her to turn from her cooking to other matters. By the mid-1930s, roughly 90% of urban households cooked by gas using lightweight utensils of enamelled sheet iron or aluminium.

Following the creation of the National Grid in 1926, the domestic use of electricity increased considerably between the wars. In 1910, only 2% of British homes had electricity but by 1935 the figure had risen to 75%. Electricity finally emerged as a practicable alternative to cooking by gas. Following the lead of the gas companies, electric cookers, like the Jackson 'P5J' of 1934, finished in white and mottled grey enamel, were hired out by the electricity boards on affordable weekly rents. But some users, unaccustomed to the slowness of heating water on electric cookers acquired small portable gas rings to boil water more quickly – and at less cost. Electricity remained the most expensive source of domestic power and whilst there were over a million households using electric cookers in 1939, this represented just 18% of homes with electricity. In the thirties, the impact of electricity was largely limited to lighting and the ownership of an electric iron. Electric toasters, washing machines and refrigerators were all available but remained luxury goods until the 1950s. Milk and fresh food was more likely to be stored inside earthenware 'coolers' or in wooden meat safes.

From the 1920s, cooking was simplified and the choice of

foods widened through the sale of foods ready for the table or near to table readiness. The complicated processes of making blancmange, jellies and other sweets were reduced to a single short operation by the use of prepared powders. American-style cereals taken with milk and sugar became popular. The range of canned foods introduced by Heinze, Cross & Blackwell and others also expanded enormously. In 1919, soup, salmon, corned beef and Californian fruits were the only choice but by the thirties almost every kind of domestic and foreign fruit, meat, game, fish and vegetable was available in tins at prices which most people could afford, at least occasionally. Never was the tin opener more needed.

Doing the weekly wash continued to be one of the hardest kitchen tasks facing the housewife. It usually dominated Mondays although preparations often began the previous night when the washing was sorted into separate piles and the dirtiest soaked in readiness. Early on Monday morning, the wash copper was filled, Oxydol or Rinso added to the water and then it was lit. Many 1930s households used portable gas heated coppers although coppers set in brickwork and heated by a small fire below remained common. The washing was then scrubbed with hard household soap using a wooden wash tub, a ribbed wash board or just the sink. Alternatively, it was pummelled in a galvanised iron wash tub using a three legged wooden washing dolly or a 'posser' with a copper end. The washing was then boiled and stirred with a boiler stick before being rinsed. Whites were given a final rinse with laudry blue which disguised any hint of yellow and helped the household linen look whiter than white. 'Out of the blue comes the whitest wash' was the advertising slogan of Reckits of Hull who produced their little muslin bags of 'Bag Blue' until the 1980s. 'Robin' starch was used to stiffen linens and shirt collars. Finally, the washing was folded and wrung through a mangle and then hung out to dry.

It was unremitting hard labour which had to be repeated for each type of washing, for coloureds, then the woollens and finally greasy rags. There was little time for cooking.

Bubble and squeak prepared from the cold potatoes and cabbage left over from the Sunday dinner was often served with cold meat followed, perhaps, by a rice pudding or suet pudding with jam or syrup. One women raised in a Liverpool suburb in the 1920s remembered returning home from school to, 'a damp smell compounded of steam, wet wool, Sunlight soap, bubble and squeak and rice pudding'.

★　★　★

By the mid-1930s the search for greater efficiency in the kitchen had led to the idea of a fully fitted, streamlined room with stainless steel sink and electrical appliances arranged with storage units and laminated work tops as one seamless unit. After the Second World War, these features came to typify kitchen design along with a greater reliance on electrical equipment. By 1960, the thirties kitchen, with its mottled grey enamelled cooker, kitchen cabinet and meat safe suddenly looked very old fashioned. But no sooner had modernism triumphed than a nostalgia for the traditional re-emerged. In the 1970s and 1980s, a craze in suburbia for the farmhouse and cottage look saw Formica replaced by stripped pine, Laura Ashley wall paper and lots of old stoneware jars and bottles. Today, modernism is back in fashion. The contemporary look demands fittings of light wood (but not pine) and stainless steel – and yet farmhouse kitchens retain their timeless appeal whilst kitchens in museums and historic homes attract huge audiences. There is no doubt that kitchens of all kinds continue to fascinate.